WHAT IS NFT
How to create and make money for beginners

Contents

INTRODUCTION

NFT, which stands for "Non-Fungible Tokens," are digital assets that function as unique items in a blockchain. They can represent tickets to an event, ownership of a company's shares, game cards, and much more. The beauty of NFTs is that they aren't limited by physical location and are impossible to counterfeit or copy. People have been making NFTs since 2013, but now the technology is finally catching on—and there's a tremendous opportunity for people with the skills and know-how to make money.

Anyone understanding the crypto space knows that blockchain technology is exploding across every industry. The emergence of NFTs is fueling this growth. At its core, blockchain technology enables people to exchange money, data, or anything of value in a transparent, trustless way—without a third-party intermediary like a bank. A decentralized platform makes it possible to create online markets where buyers and sellers can come together and trade directly with each other. Markets on the blockchain are made up of smart contracts that allow people who don't know each other (or even trust each other) to exchange money or other valuables.

NFT stands for "non-fungible token." Fungible means interchangeable, so non-fungible means something isn't identical to another individual item—the opposite of fungible. An example of a fungible asset is gold; every piece of gold is the same and interchangeable with another piece of gold. An example of a non-fungible asset is a vintage card from the Pokémon trading card game—each card is unique and different from all other cards.

NFTs operate just like Pokemon cards—they are unique digital assets that someone can own. NFTs are the forerunners of crypto-collectibles – digital items that are scarce and cannot be replicated or counterfeited like physical collectibles (think Beanie Babies or baseball cards) or unique digital items like digital art, web domains, or computer games.

Non-Fungible Tokens (NFTs) are specific crypto assets that can create value for people who know how to create and use them. NFTs are essentially digital items that can be traded. These items hold value in much the same way as cryptocurrencies do by being scarce and accessible.

Earning money with NFTs is a bit different than making money with cryptocurrencies or tokens. It's not so much about providing a service to others or establishing a platform that other people use — it's the act of creating and trading the items themselves. You might create NFTs (maybe you'll make something like CryptoKitties, which are digital cats that you can breed). Or you could create a site that lets people trade their NFTs for other assets (like OpenSea, which lets you trade Ethereum-based collectibles).

By using an NFT, you essentially own an asset that has value in the real world (or online). That's why it's a great way to make money.

CHAPTER 1

UNDERSTANDING NON-FUNGIBLE TOKENS

What are Non-Fungible Tokens?

A non-fungible token (NFT) is an asset that cannot be divided into more than one other token. For example, a golf club, a painting, or a silverware set are all examples of non-fungible assets. In the case of art, NFTs are typically created by artists on the blockchain to sell their work in a format impervious to counterfeits, censorship, and government interference. Users can create their own NFTs using blockchain technology and "mint" them into existence.

The idea of non-fungibility is simple once it is explained. It refers to the fact that each unit of a virtual asset has a unique identity, one that cannot be replicated or altered digitally in any way. This means that each NFT is like its own little "piece" of the universe, with a value on its own rather than as part of something greater, such as dollars off to the side of rubles.

Non-fungible tokens can be made from virtually anything tangible. For example, a physical painting or piece of artwork such as a "Mona Lisa" painting can be tokenized and then sold or used in a digital marketplace.

(The concept of non-fungibility has been well established in the traditional art market, but it is being tested out with greater success in the digital art world.)

What does NFT mean for businesses?

Non-fungible tokens can be used as certificates of authenticity, ownership, loyalty, or rewards program points. For example, a brand can tokenize its rewards points (i.e., "codify" them) and make them tradable on blockchain-based marketplaces. Businesses can also create their non-fungible digital assets to represent specific items in stock, such as shirts or suits, making it possible for owners to resell them online in exchange for cryptocurrencies such as Bitcoin and Ethereum. This would allow businesses to add value to such items before selling them, as well as make trading between users easier.

What does an NFT represent?

Non-fungible tokens can represent any physical or digital asset. Businesses can create non-fungible tokens to represent their products, brand, or services. This is done by associating the token with certain attributes of the asset (its size, color, etc.), which gives users a variety of information about it. For example, a producer of bottled water can create 100 NFTs to represent their products and associate each token with the location, size, quality (number of calories), color, and so on. This data can be used to gain a better understanding of the product and to speed up transactions.

Because NFTs are unique and like their own little pieces of the universe, they should not be confused with fungible tokens, which have one value (i.e., money). Even though fungible and non-fungible are both types of tokens, fungible tokens are still governed by a single power (i.e., one issuer or central authority in charge of the ledger). This means that all fungibles are already interchangeable, making them better for use as currency. Non-fungibles can never be exchanged at face value because their values cannot be easily altered or copied, making it impossible to "trade" them out of existence.

CHAPTER 2

HOW TO CREATE AN NFT

Creating non-fungible tokens is not difficult, especially when there are many free tools online that allow users to create and launch their NFTs with little to no programming experience.

The number of tools for non-fungible tokens has grown over time to the point where it is possible to create these tokens without using a single line of code.

In the past, developers had to rely on either ERC-721 or ERC-20 tokens, basically two types of tokens. Using these older standards, developers were required to create a smart contract using Ethereum's network for each new token they wanted to release. On the other hand, NFTs do not require that level of programming knowledge, as users can use a browser-based tool to create them.

What is an ERC-20 token?

An ERC-20 token is a standard form of tokens used in the Ethereum network to define a new asset. They can be used in all Ethereum-based platforms, but they do not have the same features as non-fungible tokens.

For example, ERC-20 tokens are fungible, but they do not have a single point of accountability. Since you can create an unlimited number of ERC-20 tokens, it is difficult to determine the true owner of each token. On the other hand, NFTs only need one identifier: the non-fungible identifier, which is a unique token that identifies each token.

The need to build smart contracts is eliminated when creating NFTs in most platforms, as the process involves only one line of code. Thanks to the lack of programming knowledge required to create an NFT, most platforms can handle the transaction of non-fungible tokens for crypto exchanges.

Where to get ERC20 smart contract templates

Since Ethereum is the most popular blockchain, its tokens are usually used to benchmark new assets. The ERC-20 is currently one of the most commonly used smart contract templates in Ethereum. It allows developers to deploy their tokens in a secure way that can be verified and easily deployed.

You can find many free ERC-20 smart contract templates on Github, or you can use a service such as OpenZeppelin to do so.

Like any other smart contract, users are not required to complete coding tasks to create an ERC-20 token. Most of the time, it requires only one line of code. Because of this feature, you can conveniently find a button on many Ethereum-based websites that allow you to create your first NFTs without having programming experience.

How to Make an NFT

Once you have all of the items above, go to a place on the web that allows you to create NFTs. There are many places to make NFTs online. A good example is Novusphere. To make an NFT, follow these steps:

1. Choose your item

Let's start from the beginning. If you haven't already, you'll need to figure out what unique digital asset you want to turn into an NFT. It could be a custom painting, photograph, song, collectible video game, meme, GIF, or even a tweet. An NFT is a one-of-a-kind digital item with only one owner. The NFT value is determined by rarity.

Before you start, double-check that you own the intellectual property rights to the item you want to turn into an NFT. If you make an NFT for a digital asset you don't own, you could face legal consequences.

2. Choose your blockchain

Next, take a look at the blockchain you'll use to create your non-fungible token.

Many blockchains support NFTs nowadays. Even if it is impossible to collaborate with another blockchain, you can still use its tokens in other projects that already support it as a currency.

To simplify the process, search for "ERC-20 token" on the official website of each blockchain to discover which one is compatible with NFTs. It will display a page listing assets listed on each chain and their trade value on secondary markets.

The most popular and commonly used blockchains are the Ethereum blockchain, the Cardano blockchain, and the NEO blockchain.

3. Choose your wallet

You'll need a wallet for your NFT to transact with it successfully once you create it. A wallet is an online program that allows users to interact with their cryptocurrency through smart contracts. To find the right wallet for NFTs, you can use a search engine like Google. If you want to create non-fungible tokens, try Bancor, Meta Mask, and MyEtherWallet.

You'll want to buy some cryptocurrency once you've set up your digital wallet. Most NFT platforms accept Ether, the Ethereum blockchain platform's cryptocurrency. If you already have cryptocurrency, you'll want to link it to your digital wallet so that you can create and sell NFTs with it.

4. Choose your NFT market

It's time to start creating (and hopefully selling) your NFT once you have a digital wallet and some cryptocurrency. For this, you'll need to select an NFT marketplace. OpenSea, CryptoKitties, and RareBits are some of the most popular NFT marketplaces. You can create, buy, and sell NFTs on these marketplaces. You'll need to research each NFT marketplace to learn about its audience and other details in order to find a platform that's a good fit for your NFT. You'll need to link your NFT marketplace to your digital wallet after you've chosen it. This will allow you to pay the fees associated with minting your NFT and keep any sales proceeds.

5. Upload your asset

With your digital wallet, NFT marketplace, and cryptocurrency ready for action, the final step is to upload your asset file. If you don't already have an NFT, this step can be difficult. Some NFT marketplaces allow you to upload .png, .jpg, .svg, or other assets as long as they're over 100KB. Most accept only images or videos in one of these formats. And though a single-colored image or video file doesn't need to be transparent for it to work as an NFT, it's strongly recommended that you make your digital asset transparent or invisible so that users can see whatever is behind it without obstruction.

The .png format is also popular for NFTs. In this format, colors will be represented as hexadecimal numbers. The colors at the very bottom of the screen are just a sample of the colors found in your NFT. If you want to create an NFT that's completely black, your original image should be in the color of #000000 or any other color on this scale. If you want to create an NFT with no color, your original image should be in a blank space. If it still has an image within it, that part of the asset won't work as an NFT because there will be an invisible space where whatever image is inside can still be seen by users.

6. Choose your price and sell it

The final step is to select a price for your NFT. Some NFT marketplaces offer you two options: free or bought. Suppose you want to make an NFT that's free. In that case, the platform will automatically supply it with random numbers (called "nonces") until it's unique enough to be distinguishable from any other asset on its blockchain. Free NFTs are useful for creating as many as you want without having to pay transaction fees, but they're not necessarily worth anything in the long run. Their value may even drop over time because of the limited amount being traded across secondary markets.

You can create your NFT for a different price if you don't want to pay for it. If you want to create an NFT worth more, you need to use the buy option. The buy option allows you to select the price your item is worth. This is the same as selling it on an existing marketplace that charges transaction fees and will send those fees your way if you choose this option. In this case, there's no need to upload the asset file and choose a free or bought price when creating an NFT because the platform will do this automatically for you, given the price you select.

CHAPTER 3

HOW TO MANAGE AND TRADE NON-FUNGIBLE TOKENS

Once your NFT is created, you can view your crypto wallet to see its value and convert it into fiat currency. You'll also need to understand how to manage, store, and trade your NFT.

Have a personal or business account on the blockchain where you created it

Take a look at each platform's official website to learn more about it. This will explain who it is made for and whether or not they have their cryptocurrency that can be stored in their wallets using other blockchains like Ethereum or NEO. You'll also learn who owns each platform's technology behind the scenes so that you can make sure there are no security risks involved.

Select which blockchain you want to use to store and trade your NFTs

No matter which crypto platform you decide to use, you will need to have a wallet that is compatible with that specific blockchain. Blockchain wallets are just like normal software wallets—everything is stored in one place rather than the blockchain holding your information. This way, your information stays private and secure at all times.

Make sure that the blockchain you choose is secure and trustworthy

These three considerations will aid you in determining whether or not to store your NFT on that platform. The first one is security. If it is easy to steal instead of protecting, it's going to be a bad idea. You should look over their official websites to make sure there haven't been any recent security breaches or hacks. The second thing is trustworthiness. This can also be determined by checking the websites of each platform to see if they have done anything wrong in the past years and how they were able to recover from them, as well as their community's opinion on them.

The third thing that should be checked is whether or not the platform has a privacy policy for any transactions you do. Because banking and personal data are encrypted and stored on a blockchain, it's always a good idea to double-check that your information is safe. Don't let anyone else steal your crypto from you.

Search for the nearest exchange that offers crypto-to-crypto trading

To buy and sell NFTs without fiat currency being involved, you need to have an exchange to trade them in. These exchanges can be traded against other currencies or used as storage wallets where you can store your NFTs. They are often considered decentralized exchanges (DEX) since they use smart contracts to execute transactions on the blockchain.

Read their Terms and Conditions

One way to determine if an exchange is credible is through its terms and conditions. You can find these on their home page or their website's footer. It doesn't matter if you fully comprehend everything that is written there; what matters is that you read it thoroughly enough to avoid being duped. If anything doesn't add up or feel right, don't put your money into it.

If you are using a personal or business account, you'll have to opt for a wallet that integrates the exchange and is compatible with it. If not, your transaction might be lost forever.

Find out how much speed there is in the block's confirmation time

The faster your transaction will be processed and reflected in your wallet's control panel, the more speed there is on an exchange. The SEC and CFTC released reports that suggest that it might take up to two weeks to process an order if it involves fiat currency (rather than crypto). When dealing with NFTs, you can expect instant transactions when they are inputted into the exchange's system.

By using these simple techniques, you can now start trading NFTs. The tips above will help you understand how to create and trade your non-fungible tokens and manage them.

CHAPTER 4

TOKENIZATION OF REAL-WORLD ASSETS

Businesses are increasingly adopting blockchain technology. The use of smart contracts has become a popular topic in the workplace.

The blockchain industry is still in its infancy, and numerous exciting new projects are expected to emerge as people learn how to use blockchain technology. Some companies may see this new way of creating value as a threat to their business, motivating them to develop unique blockchain technology to avoid potential risks.

The security token process

Based on the research and work done by the industry experts, there are two main ways in which security tokens can be issued:

Initial coin offering (ICO)

It is similar to the ERC-20 process but simplifies it to make it easier for the investor. The buyer should acquire an ownership position in the company behind the token instead of just getting a utility token. The company is more likely to be more active in the digital world and have a larger customer base.

Security token offering (STO)

It is similar to an ICO, except it does not use tokens. STOs allow for the issuance of security tokens in response to regulatory requirements rather than a party's desire to raise capital. This means that businesses avoid additional fees and losses from investors by selling their security assets directly to them rather than through a smart contract, benefiting from both the discounted sales price and lower overall costs associated with an ICO process.

The usage of both ICOs and STOs has its pros and cons, and it is important to compare the main differences between these two keenly.

STO vs. ICO

STOs are more complicated to create and frequently require the assistance of a seasoned blockchain firm or law firm with experience in these types of offerings. However, they are likely to comply with regulatory requirements and be legally compliant.

ICO is a faster way of raising funding, as it does not involve any regulatory requirements and is a cheaper way of raising funds. The returns may be lower than STOs but are often higher than other traditional investment opportunities.

The tokenization of real-life assets

The next big trend is the tokenization of real-world assets such as art, collectibles, cars, real estate, precious metals, etc. This new concept can help bridge the gap between traditional digital assets and real-world assets.

One of the main benefits of tokenizing physical goods is that it gives these products' digital life. For example, a painting can be used as an art piece that can be traded on a blockchain with other users or even used as collateral on loan or taken out in exchange for goods when trading cryptocurrencies.

This could make digital art an integral part of the overall financial system and create an entirely new marketplace for people to trade otherwise worthless artworks.

Many people are convinced that blockchain technology can effectively change data stored on computer systems. Blockchain's ledger system guarantees transparency and security from data tampering and deletion. In addition, it has been shown that this new technology can help reduce cross-border payments time and costs and minimize fraud.

The three main categories of blockchain technology are private chain, consortium chain, and public chain.

A private chain is a limited set of nodes working together to protect a network's privacy, security, and integrity. These private chains do not require centralized control or governance mechanisms to manage consensus across participants in the network. In addition, they can add or remove nodes as needed without changing the basic unit of the blockchain.

Private chains typically serve a single business purpose such as supply chain management, payroll, etc. They often come with a closed-loop architecture, which means that all transactions are carried out and recorded within the chain and are only accessible to participants in the network.

Private versus public chain

Private chains can be built on existing public blockchains like Ethereum or NEO. However, even though public chains offer transparency and wide participation in their users, private chains allow greater control over access rights and protection from cybersecurity threats.

A public chain is a public ledger shared among users of nodes. It decentralizes operations and provides transparency, accountability, and security. It can be used to build private chains on top of its network.

Consortium chains have been created to operate in a private environment but are also open to the public through smart contracts. Distributed applications built on top of consortium chains can use their open, decentralized structure without compromising privacy or security. Unlike private blockchains with a limited number of nodes, consortium chains have unlimited nodes spread worldwide.

Consortium chains use different consensus mechanisms. They can use Proof-of-Stake (PoS) or Proof-of-Authority (PoA), which results in faster and more efficient transactions, effective scalability, and lower transaction processing costs than other public chain types.

Blockchain technology is now being used in many industries to improve efficiency in the supply chain system. This includes creating new connections between companies, offering solutions to make transparency and security happen within the supply chain industry, and creating a better tracking system for products as they move through the different stages of their manufacturing process. It also offers companies new ways to do business.

CHAPTER 5

HOW TO FIND YOUR FIRST NFT TOKENS TO INVEST IN

The majority of ICOs are not worth investing in. The whole concept is comprised of artificial costs and unwarranted returns. The top 20% or so ICOs will probably become the next big crypto-trend, while the other 80% or so will fade away into obscurity.

To determine which ones are worth it, you need to determine which companies utilize the technology and have a promising future. To do this, you need to look at the numbers and see which ones have more value than traditional investments like stocks and bonds.

The thing to remember is that not all crypto-tokens are created equal. Many different NFTs are available on the market, and some will do better than others. It is important to find the tokens with a real-world value and make sense as a long-term investment. One of the factors why initial coin offerings (ICOs) have become so popular since the market crash, but also why so many of them have failed.

Finding Your First NFT Tokens To Invest In

When choosing which tokens you want to invest in, consider several things. Generally, though, they should have a real value or be backed by something tangible like gold or land to generate a sustainable income stream. This will allow the tokens to appreciate and keep you from losing money.

Do you want security tokens or non-security tokens? The answer depends on your plans and how much risk you want to take.

Many people choose security tokens because they want to invest in companies they are familiar with, such as stocks and bonds. However, because selling NFT securities can be difficult, increasing the risk of losing money may not be the best option. Non-security tokens are easier to sell and transfer because they usually follow the ERC721 standard. All you need to do is transfer the ownership of the token to a smart contract, and that's it.

The coin you choose will depend on your risk tolerance. If you are afraid of losing money, non-security tokens are probably a better choice. A coin that offers potential for long-term growth is ideal security. This could be related to the price or the technology behind it, such as utility tokens used in an app or tokenized real estate properties.

Most people want to invest in something backed by tangible assets because it provides them with steady income every month and keeps their crypto safe from any potential loss.

How to Find the Best NFT Tokens to Invest In

There are many things to consider when finding the best tokens to invest in, but there are also ways to navigate this process. Below you will find some steps and examples of picking the right tokens.

1. Pick A Good Cryptocurrency Exchange

Choosing the appropriate cryptocurrency exchange is one of the most critical decisions an investor can make. Most people will choose a cryptocurrency exchange because it's easy and convenient, but these exchanges have high fees and are usually bad. One of the best options is KuCoin, but others provide better services for holders like Cobinhood, Binance, and Huobi.

Depending on how much you plan to invest, you need to choose a good exchange. Most exchanges will have a fee of at least 0.1% per transaction, but some exchanges can be more expensive because they demand higher fees. KuCoin is by far the best option because they charge only 0.2% trading fee and 0.1% withdrawal fee, which is the lowest out of any other exchange in the world today.

Another consideration when choosing an exchange is its trading volume (extremely low), as this may allow for price manipulation or pump-and-dump schemes by unscrupulous investors. Some exchanges with low trading volume are RawByte, KuCoin, and BitForex. You can check the 24-hour trading volume on CoinMarketCap.

2. Choose Your Type of Coin

The next step is to choose a coin to invest in based on your risk tolerance and investment objectives. There are multiple types of coins, including security tokens, non-security tokens, and more. Depending on how much risk you're willing to take with your investment, some coins will be better than others.

Most people want to invest in security tokens because they are backed by assets and provide regular income streams. The main problem with security tokens is that it can be difficult to sell them if you don't want to keep them forever. This can result in losing money, so you need to research and find the right coins while considering the risks.

3. Look For Low Trading Volume or Extraordinary Low

When selecting a coin, you need to watch for extraordinarily low trading volume, especially when it comes from smaller exchanges like BitForex's and Raw Byte's. If people are dumping their token, you will have a lower value than expected from the market. This can also result in price manipulation so that you get fewer shares than you should.

Second, you will have to ensure the exchange has a low trading volume. Generally, exchanges with low volume are bad because it's easy for traders to manipulate the price and make trades without a need to show their real identity on trading platforms. It's recommended to only use KuCoin, Binance, and Huobi because they have low volumes that don't allow price manipulation or pump-and-dump schemes.

4. Watch Out For Airdrops

Another thing to watch out for is airdrops because this is how scammers try to scam people. Scam artists will devise ways of getting your private keys so they can steal your tokens. However, you can get around this by only keeping your funds in secure wallets like Ledger or Trezor, where you control the private keys. Check the official website and social media accounts of the NFT project to make sure it's legitimate before taking any action.

5. Determining the Utility of the Coin

Investing in an NFT token can be risky, but you need to ensure the coin has utility before choosing one. Because all of these will have a different price and marketability, you need to evaluate which is most useful for your purposes. It's best to pick a coin backed by something and provide value or service. You can find the utility behind NFT tokens by looking at their whitepaper and their team or past projects.

How to manage risk and profit in a long-term manner

If you are investing in NFTs, you need to manage risk. There are two ways to do this:

Diversify your portfolio

When it comes to investing in digital assets, you will want to diversify your portfolio to not concentrate on one or two coins. This is the safest method of risk management, as it will protect your investment from market downturns and price fluctuations. Most cryptocurrency investors diversify their portfolios across many coins, while some stick with just one or two coins. Using a technique known as dollar-cost averaging is the most efficient method (DCA). DCA involves spreading out purchases over time instead of putting all of your money into it at once. The latter is called lump-sum investing, and it can result in big losses if you buy high.

Watch the market and avoid manipulating price strategies

The market can fluctuate a lot because of rumors or unexpected news when it comes to cryptocurrency. Investors know this, and some people will take advantage of it by manipulating prices on smaller exchanges. One strategy is to place buy orders for an NFT and then cancel them once the price has increased sufficiently to enable them to sell at a higher price point. Some unscrupulous investors will do this to take advantage of amateur investors who don't have time to sit behind their computers all day watching the market.

The "Crypto crash" of 2018 has caused investors to lose millions of dollars in cryptocurrencies, so you need to evaluate how much risk you are willing to take with your investment. The best way is to keep your coins in a secure wallet like Ledger or Trezor because if the hackers get your private keys, they will be able to steal all of your NFTs. You can also use a reputable exchange like KuCoin and

BitForex because their volumes are low, so manipulations and price manipulation cannot affect the market price as much.

CHAPTER 6

HOW TO CONVERT NFT INTO FIAT CURRENCY ON EXCHANGES

The conversion of NFTs into fiat currency is another important thing to consider. Many exchanges don't accept fiat currency, so you need to find one that does and doesn't charge a high fee for the exchange. Fiat currency is money that is used to purchase goods and services. Here are a few things you should know about converting your NFTs into fiat currency:

1. Convert to Bitcoin

Suppose you want to know how to convert NFTs into fiat currency. In that case, you should convert them into Bitcoin first because this is the most liquid cryptocurrency and, therefore, easiest to convert into fiat currency quickly. You can then exchange your Bitcoins for fiat currency on an exchange like Coinbase Pro or Binance if you want. This is the only way to get fiat currency securely and quickly.

2. Choose a reputable exchange for converting your NFTs into fiat currency

Although Coinbase has announced support for ERC20 tokens, it does not currently offer to trade Ethereum-based coins, so this is not an option yet. When using an exchange to convert your NFTs into fiat currency, you need to ensure that the exchange does not have any hidden transaction or conversion fees. Furthermore, it would help if you looked for exchanges like Binance and KuCoin that charge a low fee but are professional exchanges with proven security and a good reputation in the community.

3. Convert NFTs into fiat currency when the value is at its lowest

When choosing an exchange, you should look for one that provides the best rates when converting your NFTs into fiat currency. It would be beneficial if you looked for news about these assets and currencies as well, so you would know when the value of your asset is low, and you could convert it into fiat currency at a good rate. It's also important to know that most exchanges have a daily limit on how much they will convert from your assets or coins to fiat currency. If you're going to need more than this, you might want to consider transferring your assets or coins to another exchange.

4. Consider trading your NFTs for a market cap of more than $1 billion

If you have a small market cap, you might have to wait a few hours or days before your NFT is accepted for conversion into fiat currency. However, if you have a larger asset with a high market cap, you might find it faster. You're also likely to convert your NFTs at a better rate since more volume will be on the exchange.

5. Study the network fee

The network fee from the exchange can vary from one exchange to another, so you need to know the fees before you start trading. For example, Binance charges a flat 0.1% for each transaction on cryptocurrency-to-cryptocurrency transactions. Keep in mind that larger market cap assets might take longer to convert and involve more currency and more money if you want a better rate. Therefore, if you have an asset with a higher market cap and higher value than a smaller asset, it might be better to wait until your assets are worth more instead of converting them into fiat currency right away.

List of the exchanges where you can convert NFTs into fiat currency

Waves DEX

This is a decentralized exchange like Binance and Kucoin. Still, it allows users to convert NFT into fiat currency by sending assets to their e-wallet and redeeming them for fiat currency (e.g., USD) via an external gateway. This took place in the Waves network and was created by the Waves team. It's a very secure cryptocurrency exchange that features fast transactions with low fees for trading assets on its network.

Binance

A Cryptocurrency exchange with a trading platform similar to traditional exchanges. It features more than 200 cryptocurrencies and charges a flat 0.1% for each transaction on cryptocurrency-to-cryptocurrency transactions.

KuCoin

Another cryptocurrency exchange allows users to trade most major cryptocurrencies, tokens, and digital assets. Some of the coins you can find on this exchange include NEO, LTC, ETH, BTC, and many others. The KuCoin platform offers flat transaction fees that range from 0%-0.2%, depending on your asset purchase size.

The Bancor Protocol

The Bancor Protocol is different from other cryptocurrency exchanges. It converts NFTs directly into Ethereum or any ERC20 compatible tokens and charges no fee for this transaction. However, before using the Bancor protocol to convert your assets or coins, you need to create an account on their platform. Sending a message to the Bancor Network Contract with your network wallet's address, the destination Bancor wallet's address, and the amount of NFT you want to convert is all it takes.

Rocketr

This is the only cryptocurrency exchange that doesn't charge a fee to convert your assets or coins. Rocketr also has a fiat currency gateway to make these conversions quickly, but they currently allow users to convert only Bitcoin and Ether. If you want to use this service, you must first create an account on the platform and link your bank account with it.

How to convert or sell your ERC20 or Ethereum exchange accounts into real money or security token

Since there are now more than 1,000 cryptocurrency exchanges and trading platforms operating globally, it is not easy to know where to sell your Ethereum-based coins or tokens. That's why you need to consider the following points before making a decision:

- Where do I convert my assets and coins?
- Do I have to pay more than 10% when converting my assets into real money?
- How can I get my converted money for free?

If you want to convert your assets or coins into real money, the best way is to use an exchange like Poloniex, Bittrex, Bitfinex, and other more professional exchange platforms. However, these exchanges are rather expensive and have high transaction fees. It can cost a few dollars when converting your assets or coins into real money. As a result, this is not the best option if you will sell

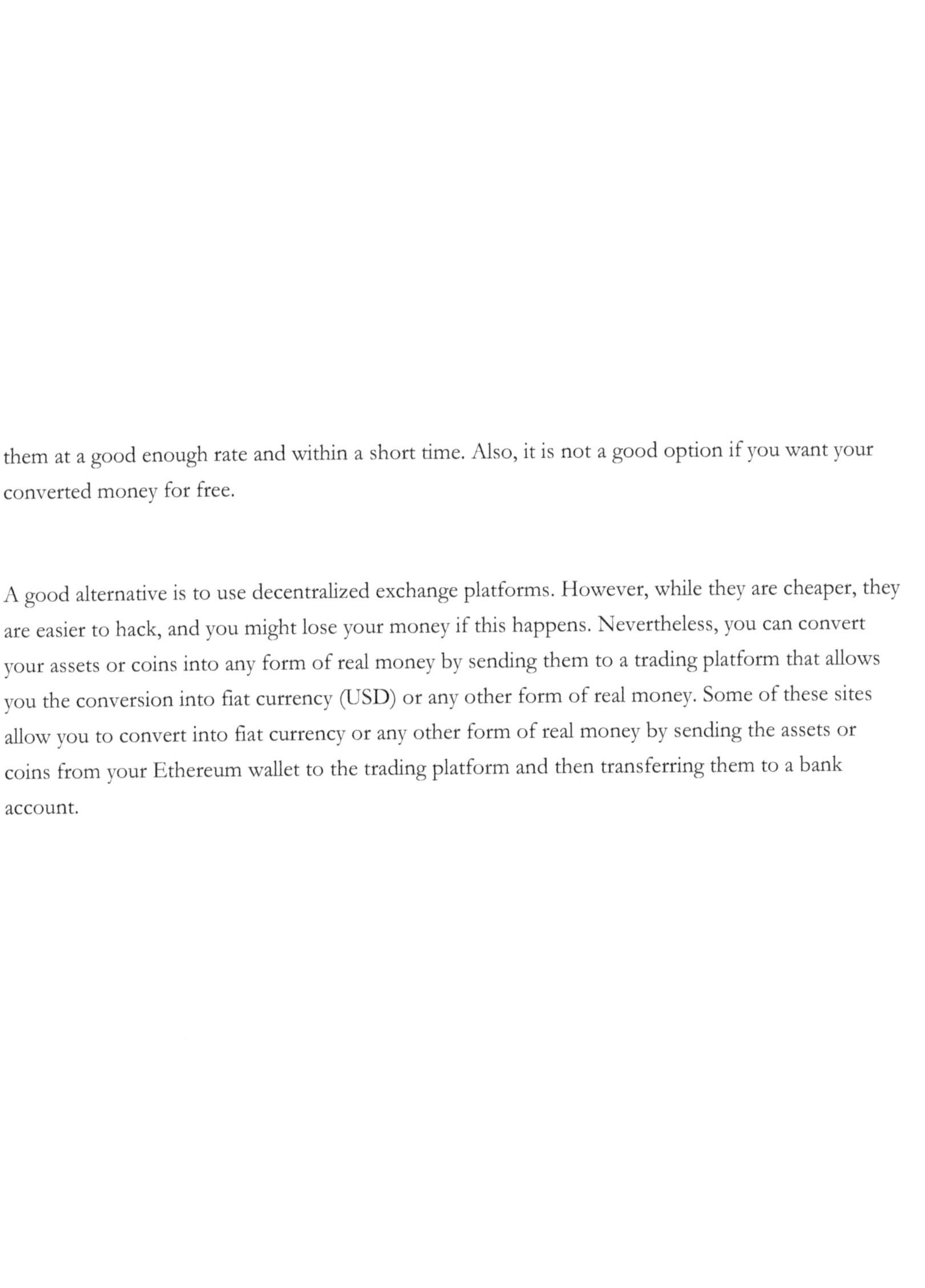

them at a good enough rate and within a short time. Also, it is not a good option if you want your converted money for free.

A good alternative is to use decentralized exchange platforms. However, while they are cheaper, they are easier to hack, and you might lose your money if this happens. Nevertheless, you can convert your assets or coins into any form of real money by sending them to a trading platform that allows you the conversion into fiat currency (USD) or any other form of real money. Some of these sites allow you to convert into fiat currency or any other form of real money by sending the assets or coins from your Ethereum wallet to the trading platform and then transferring them to a bank account.

CONCLUSION

As NFTs become more popular, their sale prices are rising. As a result, NFT creators stand to profit handsomely. Given the fees associated with minting and selling NFTs, not all NFTs will even sell, let alone make their creator any money. You should budget for the possibility of losing money on your NFT creation due to the costs. Selling an NFT valuable to others and setting a minimum price that will more than cover any associated fees is the best way to avoid a loss. You also should be prepared for the possibility of making a loss on an NFT. The other option is to create an NFT that you will not want to sell but perhaps give away as a reward or for other reasons.

Additionally, once you create your own NFT and set up the rules surrounding its use, you need to consider if your digital asset has the possibility of being sold at a higher price in the future. If so, then you might want to plan a way that allows others to buy your assets at a lower price now while they can still get them before their prices rise further. Otherwise, set a price that makes sense relative to your goals as they relate to this token sale.

Whatever your reason for creating an NFT, the most important thing is to create one valuable to others. The goal here is to make a profit by selling it at a good enough price and to have something that people will want to buy. The best way to do this is to create a coin or token that people can use and get value from.

You should know that many NFTs are selling for more than their original creators expected when they created them. This is because the price of these tokens has increased over time, which means their creators stand to profit handsomely in the future. Therefore, you should spend time and effort creating NFTs that can become valuable to others over time.

Although creating an NFT is relatively easy, creating one valuable to others can be difficult. In addition, NFTs are not created equally. Because of the current scarcity of new coins and tokens, many investors don't know where and how to buy these digital assets when they want to invest in them. Also, a lack of regulation has made it easier for scammers and fraudsters to create fake NFTs or stolen NFTs that actors want to cash out from investors by offering fake investments with their NFTs. Therefore, you need to be cautious and research before buying and selling NFTs.

NFTs will continue to grow in popularity as more people realize their value. As a result, the blockchain community at large needs to grow its understanding of what NFTs are with regard to both their creation and use. As this understanding grows, so will the NFT market and its potential to impact online commerce and economics in many ways.